ANIMAL LIVES

Birds

WORLD
BOOK

a Scott Fetzer company

Chicago

www.worldbook.com

World Book, Inc.
233 N. Michigan Avenue
Chicago, IL 60601
U.S.A.

For information about other World Book publications, visit our Web site at **http://www.worldbook.com** or call **1-800-WORLDBK (967-5325)**.

For information about sales to schools and libraries, call **1-800-975-3250 (United States),** or **1-800-837-5365 (Canada)**.

Editorial:

Editor in Chief: Paul A. Kobasa
Project Manager: Cassie Mayer
Writer: Brian Johnson
Researcher: Jacqueline Jasek
Manager, Contracts & Compliance
 (Rights & Permissions): Loranne K. Shields
Indexer: David Pofelski

Graphics and Design:

Manager: Tom Evans
Coordinator, Design Development
 and Production: Brenda B. Tropinski
Book design by: Don Di Sante
Photographs Editor: Kathy Creech
Senior Cartographer: John Rejba

Pre-Press and Manufacturing:

Director: Carma Fazio
Manufacturing Manager: Steven K. Hueppchen
Senior Production Manager: Jan Rossing

Picture Acknowledgments:

Front Cover: © Pete Oxford, Minden Pictures;
Back Cover: © Igorsky/ Shutterstock

© Angela Hampton Picture Library/Alamy Images 43; © Arco Images/Alamy Images 10; © Arctic Images/Alamy Images 39; © Ross Armstrong, Alamy Images 33; © blickwinkel/Alamy Images 9, 22, 25; © Danita Delimont/Alamy Images 27; © Tim Graham, Alamy Images 32; © Christian Kapteyn, Alamy Images 32; © Don Kates, Alamy Images 40-41; © Natural Visions/Alamy Images 29; © Norman Price, Alamy Images 37; © Robert Scholl, Alamy Images 21; © Robert Shantz, Alamy Images 24; © Paul & Joyce Berquist, Animals Animals 30; © Richard Wagner, Animals Animals 31; AP/Wide World 40; © Wolfgang Bayer, Discovery Channel Images/Getty Images 6; © De Agostini Picture Library/Getty Images 17; © James Hager, Robert Harding World Imagery/Getty Images 27; © Tim Laman, National Geographic/Getty Images 9; © Alberto Lowe, Reuters/Landov 42; © Enrique Marcarian, Reuters/Landov 42; © Theo Allofs, Minden Pictures 12; © Tui De Roy, Minden Pictures 19, 28-29, 41; © Gerry Ellis, Minden Pictures 7; © Yva Momatiuk & John Eastcott, Minden Pictures 11; © Pete Oxford, Minden Pictures 24; © Michael Quinton, Minden Pictures 18; © Konrad Wothe, Minden Pictures 5; © Oriol Alamany, Nature Picture Library 8; © Hermann Brehm, Nature Picture Library 21; © John Cancalosi, Nature Picture Library 31; © Bruce Davidson, Nature Picture Library 26; © Rolf Nussbaumer, Nature Picture Library 4-5, © Pete Oxford, Nature Picture Library 38-39; © Constantinos Petrinos, Nature Picture Library 34; © Markus Varesvuo, Nature Picture Library 29; © Anthony Mercieca, Photo Researchers 20; © Shutterstock 4, 6, 10, 13, 14, 16-17, 18, 23, 26, 35, 36, 39, 44, 45; © SuperStock 13; © age fotostock/SuperStock 15, 16, 29, 35; © Mauritius/ SuperStock 20

All maps and illustrations are the exclusive property of World Book, Inc.

Library of Congress Cataloging-in-Publication Data

Birds / World Book.
 p. cm. -- (Animal lives)
 Includes index.
 Summary: "An introduction to birds and their physical characteristics, life cycle, behaviors, and adaptations to various habitats. Features include maps, diagrams, fun facts, glossary, resource list, and index"--Provided by publisher.
 ISBN 978-0-7166-0403-7
 1. Birds--Juvenile literature. I. World Book, Inc.
QL676.2.B626 2009
597--dc22
    2009008851

Animal Lives
Set ISBN: 978-0-7166-0401-3

Printed in China by:
Shenzhen Donnelley Printing Co., Ltd,
Guangdong Province
3rd Printing August 2013

Table of Contents

There is a glossary of terms on page 46. Terms defined in the glossary are in type **that looks like this** on their first appearance on any spread (two facing pages).

What Are Birds?

Birds are magnificent animals. They fly through the air, run on the land, and swim in the sea. Birds can be as colorful as a peacock or as dark as a raven. Some fly across whole oceans, while others cannot fly at all. Some birds are familiar, like the chickens, ducks, geese, and turkeys people raise for food. Other birds are mysterious, like the birds-of-paradise that live in warm, tropical regions.

Sandhill cranes rest at wetlands as they fly south for the winter.

Birds of a feather

All birds share certain features. For example, all birds have feathers. Birds also have wings, but not all birds can fly. All birds are **vertebrates** (animals with backbones), and they all hatch from eggs. Birds are also **warm-blooded,** which means their body temperature stays about the same no matter what the temperature is outside.

Where in the world?

Birds live all around the world in many different **habitats.** A habitat is the kind of place where an animal lives. Birds live in deserts and forests, on mountains and islands, and near fresh and salt water.

Birds like chickens are kept on farms to provide eggs and meat to human beings.

Fun Fact

Most scientists think that birds were once a kind of dinosaur. When the dinosaurs died out 65 million years ago, only the birds survived.

The balance of nature

Birds help keep the balance of nature in an area. They eat a variety of animals, like insects, mice, seeds, snakes, and worms. By eating insects and mice, birds keep these creatures from becoming too numerous. In turn, birds are eaten by many creatures, like foxes, raccoons, and snakes. Without birds to eat, these animals might starve.

Birds also help plants grow. When a bird eats berries or other fruit, it often swallows the seeds of that plant. When those seeds fall to the ground with the bird's droppings, the seeds can grow into a new plant.

Colorful birds-of-paradise live in warm, tropical regions.

What Are Features of Birds?

All birds share certain features, such as wings and feathers. These features can look different from **species** (kind of bird) to species. Each species of bird has features that help it survive in its **habitat**.

The albatross has the longest wings of any bird, helping it glide over the ocean.

Bird bodies

Most birds have bodies built for motion. Their body shape helps them fly through the air. Many bird bones are hollow and light, which also helps birds fly.

Feathers

Birds can have many different kinds of feathers. Flying birds have long flight feathers on their wings and tail. These help keep birds up in the air. Birds that live in cold places have a layer of short, soft feathers to keep them warm.

Feathers often provide **camouflage** (protective coloration) to help birds blend in with their surroundings. But some birds have brightly colored feathers to attract other birds.

Wings

All birds have wings, but they come in many different shapes and sizes. The kiwi of New Zealand is a flightless bird that has tiny wings hidden beneath its feathers. The albatross is a sea bird with huge wings that stretch more than 11 feet (3.4 meters) across!

Male cardinals are bright red to attract female cardinals.

Bills

Unlike most animals, birds have no teeth. Instead, they have bills (beaks). Birds use their bills to feed, to pick up materials for building nests, and for self-defense.

Legs

Some flying birds have short legs and can hop only a short distance. Birds that wade in water, like flamingoes, have long legs to hold them above the water.

Feet

Most birds have feet with four toes and a claw at the tip of each toe. Typically, three toes point forward, while one points back. This helps birds grip branches or other objects. Swimming birds like ducks have webs of skin connecting their toes, so their feet are like paddles.

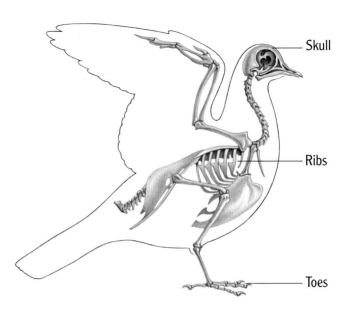

All birds have backbones. Many bones in flying birds are hollow, reducing their weight.

Wading birds like flamingoes have long, thin legs that carry them above the water.

Fun Fact

Birds come in all sizes. The bee hummingbird grows to only about 2 inches (5 centimeters) tall. The ostrich can grow up to 8 feet (2.4 meters) tall—taller than human beings!

What Senses Do Birds Have?

Like all animals, birds have senses that help them find food and escape **predators** (animals that hunt them). Birds have all five senses, but their most developed senses are sight and hearing.

Sight

Most birds have excellent eyesight. They can see more detail and more colors than people can see. Eagles, hawks, and vultures look for their food while flying high up in the sky. They have the sharpest vision of all animals.

Birds that are **nocturnal** (active at night), like most owls, have large eyes and can see well in the dark. Many diving birds like cormorants can focus equally well in the air and underwater.

Owls rely on their keen eyesight and sharp hearing to capture the animals they eat.

Hearing

Most birds have good hearing. Birds have an ear on each side of the head, but the ears cannot be seen.

Some birds have very sensitive hearing. Barn owls can hear the faintest sounds made by mice. Their hearing helps them hunt on even the darkest nights.

Taste and smell

Birds do not have a strong sense of taste, and most birds do not have a good sense of smell. But some birds do rely on their sense of smell. The kiwi hunts insects by smell. The albatross uses smell to find food out on the open ocean.

Touch

Some birds have a sharp sense of touch in their bills. A few kinds of birds hunt for insects by digging in the soil with their bills. Others use their sensitive bills to hunt fish. The roseate spoonbill uses its bill like a big scoop. It sweeps its bill through the water, snapping the bill closed when it feels a fish or other creature.

The roseate spoonbill sweeps its bill through the water, searching for fish to eat.

The kiwis of New Zealand are flightless birds that use their sense of smell to hunt insects.

Fun Fact

A few birds depend on their hearing more than their sight. South American birds called guacharos make clicking sounds that echo off the walls of the dark caves where they live. By listening to the sounds, guacharos can avoid hitting the walls.

What Do Birds Eat?

Birds eat many different things, such as insects, fish, meat, seeds, and fruit. A bird's diet depends largely on its **habitat** (the place where it lives).

Physical adaptations

The bills of birds are often **adapted** to the kinds of food they eat. Adaptations are features of a living thing that make it better able to survive and **reproduce** (make more of itself).

Insect-eaters

Birds like kiwis, swallows, and woodpeckers eat mainly insects and worms. Birds that eat insects tend to have long, skinny bills for digging in the soil.

Birds that eat insects or worms tend to have skinny bills.

Fish-eaters

Many birds, including cormorants, herons, kingfishers, and pelicans, eat fish. Some fish-eating birds have large bills that resemble scoops. Others have sharp bills useful for spearing fish.

Meat-eaters

Some of the largest birds eat meat and are called **birds of prey.** Birds of prey include eagles, falcons, hawks, owls, and vultures. They feed on birds, rodents, and snakes. These birds have broad, powerful wings and excellent eyesight. Their strong feet and sharp **talons** (claws) help them hold their victims in place. **Scavengers** like vultures eat mainly the remains of dead animals. In this way, vultures help break down animal remains and maintain the balance of nature.

Birds that eat fruit and nuts have rugged bills.

Plant-eaters

Birds like buntings, finches, parakeets, and sparrows eat mainly seeds. Birds that eat seeds tend to have short, conelike bills that are useful for cracking open tough nuts.

Some of the most colorful birds, including hornbills, parrots, and toucans, eat fruit. Most fruit-eating birds live in the warm regions of the world, where fruit is plentiful the year around.

A few birds feed mainly on the nectar (sugary liquid) produced by flowers. These birds include honeyeaters and hummingbirds. Other birds, like ducks, geese, and swans, may eat plants like grass and seaweed.

Fun Fact

The peregrine falcon is the fastest animal in the world. It has been clocked at speeds over 200 miles per hour (320 kilometers per hour) while diving! Peregrine falcons hunt other birds by swooping down and knocking them from the sky.

A bald eagle plucks a fish from the water, clutching it with sharp talons.

How Do Birds Grow?

All birds go through similar stages of development, from the time they hatch from an egg to the time they grow into adult birds. Together, these stages make up a bird's **life cycle**.

Male peacocks display their colorful tail feathers to impress females.

Courtship

In order to make baby birds, male and female birds must get together to **reproduce**. This period of time is called mating. It usually begins with the male claiming an area of land, called a **territory**.

The male tries to attract a female with **courtship** displays so she will choose him as a partner. These displays often involve dancing or building nests. Some males try to impress females with their colorful feathers. Male songbirds try to impress females with their songs.

Laying Eggs

After a bird finds a mate (partner), the birds build a nest. The female bird then lays eggs. Birds usually lay two to eight eggs a season. Eggs may be plain or spotted, pale or colored, and small or large. The parents usually **incubate** (sit on) the eggs to keep them warm. In many **species,** each parent takes turns sitting on the eggs. After 10 to 80 days, the eggs are ready to hatch.

Baby Chicks

Many newborn chicks (young) are blind, nearly featherless, and so weak they can hardly stand. They beg for food from their parents and eat to gain strength. Some chicks hatch ready to leave the nest within hours.

Newborn robin chicks cannot leave the nest until they are strong enough to survive on their own.

All birds that fly do so without being taught. But birds usually need months of practice to become skilled fliers.

Bird parents offer food, warmth, and protection to their chicks.

Fun Fact

Male satin bowerbirds build a fancy home to attract female birds. They decorate their nest with flowers, berries, and shiny objects. When a female approaches, the male spreads his wings and dances to bring attention to his gift.

Do Birds Build Homes?

Most birds build nests. Nests give birds a place to rest, to lay eggs, and to raise chicks. Many nests are in trees, but birds also build nests on the ground, in bushes, on rocky ledges, or in caves. Most bird nests are shaped like bowls or saucers.

Woodpeckers nest in the holes they create in trees.

Nest materials

Most birds build their nests out of grass, leaves, twigs, or other plant material. Blue jays and American robins use mud to glue plant materials together. Hummingbirds use spider webs. Swifts use their own thick, gummy saliva.

Unusual nests

Some birds build other kinds of nests. Certain swallows build nests made almost entirely out of mud. These nests are completely enclosed except for a small entrance. Some birds, like the monk parakeet, build enormous community nests made up of many "apartments."

Weaverbirds build hanging nests by weaving grass and twigs together.

Nestless birds

Many kinds of birds do not build nests. Woodpeckers live in holes that they make in trees. Kingfishers and bank swallows dig nests in banks of sand or clay. Most falcons simply lay their eggs on the ground.

Nest stealers

Starlings are the bullies of the bird world. They prefer to build their nests in holes in trees or cliffs. If another bird has already built a nest in a good spot, the starling may simply steal the nest, driving off the other bird!

Most cuckoos also take advantage of others' nests. They sneak their eggs into the nests of other birds. When the cuckoo chicks hatch, they push the other birds' eggs and chicks out of the nest. The chicks then trick the cheated parents into feeding them!

Ospreys build the largest nests of any North American bird.

Fun Fact

Nests come in many shapes and sizes. Nests of the smallest hummingbirds measure only about 1 inch (2.5 centimeters) high. Ospreys build nests as thick as 6 feet (1.8 meters)!

Do Birds Live in Groups?

Many kinds of birds live with at least one other bird during certain times of the year. Birds also gather in large groups for certain activities, such as feeding, mating, or flying long distances. Living together in groups helps protect birds from **predators.**

Migration

Many kinds of birds gather together into groups called flocks to feed or to **migrate.** A migration is a movement from one area to another.

The flying patterns made by a flock of birds make it more difficult for predators to catch individual birds. Migrating birds like the Canada goose often form v-shaped flocks. This shape allows birds to cut through the air more easily, like a single giant wing.

Mating

Birds live with a mate (partner) during certain parts of the year. Some birds, like geese and swans, choose one mate for life. But most birds find a new mate each season.

After the female lays eggs, the male and female often work together to raise their chicks. Once the chicks leave the nest, many adult birds separate.

Mourning doves live in large groups, pairing off to mate and build nests.

Colonies

Many sea birds gather together to nest. These large groups are called **colonies.** Colonies may host only a few hundred birds, but the largest colonies host more than a million birds!

Colonies are usually located on faraway islands or rocky cliffs. This allows parents to nest without fear of animals that steal eggs, like mice. Some birds nest close together in colonies. Other birds require more room for each nest. Most birds return to the same colony year after year. During the mating season, sea bird colonies can cover entire islands. The birds hunt for fish from the ocean, raising their chicks on land.

Canada geese *(left)* form v-shaped flocks while migrating to cut through the air more easily.

Sea birds like these gulls *(below)* often gather in large colonies on faraway islands or cliffs.

How Do Birds Communicate?

Anyone who has heard a rooster calling in the morning knows that birds can make a lot of noise! Birds communicate to mark their **territory,** to find mates, and to warn other birds of danger.

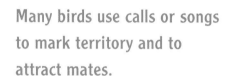

Many birds use calls or songs to mark territory and to attract mates.

Calls

Most birds have a voice that they use to call or sing. A call is usually a single sound, such as a loud squawk. Adult birds may call to attract a mate, or they may call to warn other birds that a **predator** is nearby. Chicks make high-pitched calls to tell their parents that they are hungry. Even in a crowded **colony,** parents can recognize the voice of their own chicks.

Songs

Songbirds like nightingales create songs during the mating season. Usually, only males sing. By singing from different perches, the male both marks his territory and attracts a mate. Among many **species,** males that sing the most complex songs are the most successful at mating.

The ruffed grouse makes a loud drumming sound by rapidly beating its wings.

A male frigatebird tries to impress females by inflating a bright red sac on his neck.

Drumming

Some birds make sounds in other ways. Woodpeckers make loud drumming sounds by striking their bills against trees. Drumming marks the woodpecker's territory and attracts a mate. Storks make clacking sounds with their bills during **courtship.**

Other forms of communication

In forests, birds communicate through sounds because they may have trouble seeing each other. In open areas, many bird species communicate visually. They may do so by flashing their tail feathers, raising the crest of feathers on the head, or by dancing. Unlike **mammals** and insects, very few birds communicate through odors (smells).

Fun Fact

Many birds have different calls for certain kinds of predators. Jays use one call for ground predators like cats and another call for airborne predators like hawks. Chickadees make longer alarm calls to signal more dangerous predators.

How Do Birds Hunt and Escape?

Birds have many **adaptations** that help them hunt for food and escape enemies. Adaptations like **talons** help birds hunt, while adaptations like **camouflage** help birds hide.

Hunting

Birds of prey like eagles and falcons are among the world's deadliest hunters. They use their sharp eyesight and incredible speed to swoop in on **prey** (animals that are hunted and eaten) before the victim has time to react. Their strong feet and sharp talons hold prey steady while their sharp beaks rip away hunks of flesh.

Birds of prey have different adaptations suited to their unique **habitats.** Eagles living in open areas have broad wings that allow them to stay in the air for long periods, looking for prey. Forest-dwelling hawks have shorter, more rounded wings that allow them to zip between the trees as they pursue prey.

Many birds have camouflage that helps them blend in with their surroundings.

Birds of prey like the American kestrel clutch their victims with sharp talons.

Birds that gather in flocks watch for predators with many sets of eyes.

Escaping

All but the largest birds face many threats from **predators.** If attacked, most birds do not have good defenses, so a bird's best defense is to avoid being seen. Camouflage helps many birds blend in with their surroundings. If birds are seen, they try to fly away before predators can strike.

Gathering in flocks provides birds with many sets of eyes to watch for predators. It can also make it hard for a predator to grab an individual bird.

In some cases, flocks will even fight predators. An individual sparrow stands little chance when fighting a cat. But a flock of sparrows may swoop down one after another, repeatedly striking the cat with their bills and claws. Few cats can withstand an angry flock of sparrows!

Fun Fact

A bird called the killdeer has an unusual way of defending its nest. As a predator draws near, the killdeer drags its wing along the ground, pretending to be injured. Once the killdeer has led the predator away from the nest, the bird flies off, unharmed.

Why Do Birds Migrate?

Many kinds of birds travel great distances to find food or to avoid harsh weather brought by changing seasons. During **migration,** birds may fly hours or even days without stopping to reach their new home.

Seasonal migrations

In many parts of the world, food is in short supply during certain seasons. Insects do not remain active during harsh winters. As a result, birds that feed on insects would starve if they stayed in an area with harsh winters. Instead, these birds migrate to areas where insects remain available. Birds may also migrate in search of food during the wet and dry seasons in the tropics.

Many birds travel to warmer climates in the fall. They return in the spring, when the weather warms up again. Millions of birds gather in the Arctic as the weather warms there. In the fall, these birds migrate south, before the weather turns cold.

Each year, the Arctic tern migrates from the Arctic to Antarctica and back again.

Canada geese avoid harsh winter weather by migrating south in the fall.

Fun Fact

The blackpoll warbler is a North American bird that makes one of the longest continuous migrations. It flies nonstop nearly 2,500 miles (4,000 kilometers) to its winter home in South America. The journey takes about 90 hours.

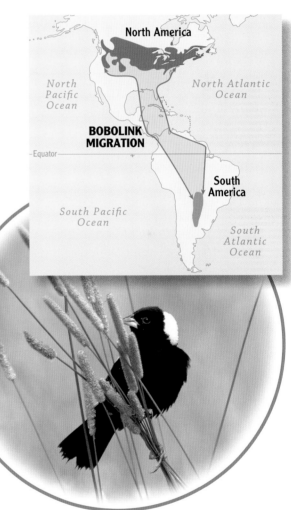

The bobolink nests in North America and flies to South America for the winter.

How birds migrate

Most migrating birds head either north or south in response to changing seasons. Some **species** of birds fly in small flocks. Others fly in flocks with many thousands of birds. Most birds migrate along the same routes (paths) each year.

Some birds migrate a fairly short distance. But others travel for weeks or even months. The Arctic tern flies all the way from the Arctic to Antarctica, only to return a few months later. Through these migrations, it travels about 22,000 miles (35,400 kilometers) in less than a year.

What Birds Live in Forests?

If you walk through a forest, you are likely to hear the sounds of many kinds of birds. The thumps of woodpeckers often echo among the trees. Many perching birds fill the air with their songs. Other birds make loud, booming calls or high-pitched shrieks. These sounds show the many kinds of birds that live in forest **habitats.**

The Clark's nutcracker uses its rugged bill to break open nuts.

Feeding on trees

Trees provide food for many birds. In turn, birds help new trees and plants grow. Some birds bury seeds for food during winter, but they may forget where they buried some seeds and leave them behind. Buried seeds may then grow into new trees in the forest.

The toucan eats mainly fruits that grow in tropical forests.

Birds that eat fruit also help trees grow. When a bird like a tropical parrot eats fruit, it also eats seeds. Those seeds are then spread to a new area of forest through the parrot's droppings.

Owls sweep through the forest in search of small creatures like mice.

Hunting birds

Many **birds of prey** live in forests, including eagles, hawks, and owls. These birds tend to have shorter, more rounded wings that allow them to zip between the trees to chase **prey**.

Owls are powerful **nocturnal** hunters that live in forests. They use their large eyes and keen hearing to hunt animals like mice and other small creatures. Their special feathers allow them to fly silently.

Other forest birds feed on animals that live in trees. Woodpeckers like the colorful yellowhammer use their sharp beaks to drill beneath tree bark to get at the insects they eat.

Fun Fact

The lyrebird is an unusual bird that lives in the forests of Australia and New Zealand. It can make the sounds of musical instruments, car alarms, and chain saws!

What Birds Live in Grasslands?

The red-billed quelea gathers in enormous flocks to feed on grain in the grasslands of Africa.

Grasslands are open areas of land with few trees. The tall grasses in these **habitats** provide cover for many birds that eat insects or seeds. The open land allows **birds of prey** to spot food from even miles away.

Open range

Because grasslands have few trees, birds' keen eyesight allows them to see across long distances. Birds of prey glide high above the land, searching for food. By gliding instead of beating their wings, they use little energy and can stay in the air for long periods.

Grassland flocks

Many grassland birds live in large flocks. This gives them more sets of eyes to watch for **predators.** Some kinds of birds gather in flocks that may contain millions of birds.

Laying low

Grasslands provide fewer places to hide than forests. When danger looms, most birds fly away. Other birds depend on their **camouflage.** When a predator approaches, these birds become perfectly still, blending in with the grass.

Runners

The largest bird alive is found in grasslands. It is the ostrich, which can reach about 8 feet (2.4 meters) tall and weigh as much as 345 pounds (156 kilograms). The ostrich cannot fly, but it has powerful legs and can run at speeds of more than 40 miles (65 kilometers) per hour. The emu of Australia and the rhea of South America are similar grassland birds.

Fun Fact

A grassland bird called the oxpecker acts as a lookout for animals like rhinos and zebras. Oxpeckers eat ticks and other creatures that dig into the skin of large **mammals.** If the oxpecker spots a predator, it flies upward and screams a warning, alerting its host to danger.

Ostriches use their powerful legs to run across grasslands.

What Birds Live on Mountains?

Life can be hard in mountain **habitats.** The temperature is colder at greater heights. The air is also thinner, making it harder to breathe. But many birds have **adapted** to life on mountains.

Peaks and cliffs

Birds have an advantage over other animals that live on mountains. Because birds can fly, they are able to ride air currents up steep cliffs that are impossible to climb. These cliffs offer great protection for the nests of mountain birds like falcons, golden eagles, and condors.

Winter coats

Some birds **migrate** to lower areas of the mountain during winter to avoid the extreme cold. Other birds have **adaptations** like thick coats of feathers that protect them from the cold. The ptarmigan (*TAHR muh guhn*) **molts** (sheds and re-grows) its summer feathers before the winter, replacing brown feathers with white ones. These feathers provide **camouflage** against snow and ice. Ptarmigan feathers grow all the way down their legs to the toes of their feet, helping to keep their feet warm.

Thin air

The air becomes thin at great heights, but special adaptations help birds breathe thin air. A system of air sacs moves each breath through a bird's lungs twice before it is released. This allows birds to get the most out of each breath.

Andean condors build nests on high cliffs that are beyond the reach of most animals.

Fun Fact

The bar-headed goose is a thin-air champ. It migrates from Tibet to its winter home in India by flying straight over the Himalaya, the tallest mountains in the world.

Ptarmigans *(below)* molt their feathers with the seasons. Their summer camouflage *(left)* blends in with rugged plants. Their winter camouflage *(right)* blends in with snow and ice.

What Birds Live in Deserts?

Deserts are dry areas that become extremely hot during the day and quite cold at night. Despite these harsh conditions, many birds have **adapted** to life in the desert.

The hot sun

Most desert birds seek shelter during the hottest part of the day to avoid the sun. These birds are active mainly at dawn or dusk. For example, Gila woodpeckers hollow out nests from large cactus plants, where they spend much of the day.

The elf owl shelters from strong desert sunlight in holes abandoned by woodpeckers.

Other birds are strictly **nocturnal,** leaving their shelters only at night. Many nocturnal owls live in the desert, including the elf owl, the smallest owl in the world. Elf owls live in cactus nests abandoned by woodpeckers.

Water

One of the great challenges facing desert birds is that there is so little water. Desert birds have developed a number of **adaptations** to save water. Many have bodies that save as much water as possible.

Many birds that live in the desert can get most or all of the water they need from the food they eat. Desert birds feed mainly on animal flesh or insects. Animal flesh and juicy insects provide plenty of water for these birds.

Desert hummingbirds

Hummingbirds that live in deserts get the water they need from nectar, a sugary liquid from plants. Hummingbirds are able to hover in place like a helicopter while feeding on nectar. Their slender bills and long tongues allow them to reach deep inside flowers for nectar.

As it feeds, a hummingbird's bill becomes covered in pollen (tiny grains made by flowers). When the hummingbird visits another flower, it leaves pollen behind. This movement of pollen from one plant to another is necessary for many plants to **reproduce.**

Hummingbirds hover in place as they feed on flower nectar, using their long, slender bills.

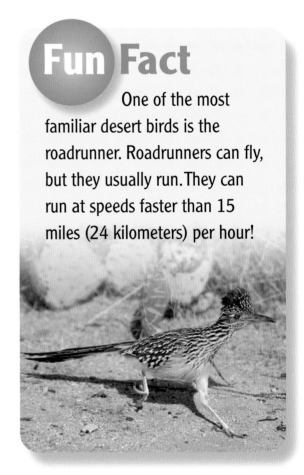

Fun Fact

One of the most familiar desert birds is the roadrunner. Roadrunners can fly, but they usually run. They can run at speeds faster than 15 miles (24 kilometers) per hour!

What Birds Live on Islands?

Islands contain many different **habitats,** ranging from shorelines to forests to mountains. Islands can be many different sizes, and some are far out in the ocean. Because birds can fly, they are often among the first animals to reach and settle islands.

Adapting to islands

After birds arrive on islands, they slowly develop **adaptations** that allow them to live in their new habitat. Birds that live on the Galapagos Islands in the Pacific Ocean show how the features of birds change as they adapt to island habitats.

Many species of finches live on the Galapagos Islands. Each species has a bill specially adapted to the kind of food it eats.

Long ago, a single kind of finch arrived on the Galapagos Islands. That finch ate seeds, but it faced little competition for other foods, like insects. Over time, at least 13 **species** of finches developed, each with a different bill suited to eating different foods. One kind of bird became many kinds.

The kea is a New Zealand mountain parrot. On islands, birds may adapt to new roles.

Birds of New Zealand

Because many islands are isolated, unusual birds can flourish. Long ago, the island country of New Zealand had no **mammals** except for bats. As a result, many species of birds developed that are found nowhere else. These include the flightless kiwis and takahes (*ta ka hees*), a rare mountain parrot called the kea (*KAY uh* or *KEE uh*), and a **nocturnal** parrot called the kakapo.

Sea bird colonies

Many sea birds gather in large **colonies** on islands to build their nests. Islands that are far from land may have no mice or other creatures that eat eggs. Many different kinds of birds often gather on the same island to nest.

Fun Fact

Birds can help bring plants to islands by carrying seeds. A bird that eats fruit carries the seeds in its body and releases them in its droppings. The seeds may then sprout into growing plants.

New Zealand is in the southwest Pacific Ocean.

The flightless takahe is among many New Zealand birds that live nowhere else.

What Birds Live on Coasts?

Coasts are seashore **habitats** that support many kinds of birds with their wealth of animal and plant life. Many birds that live there have **adaptations** that help them get food from the water. Coastal birds can also be found near lakes, swamps, and other inland waters. These birds are often called **waterfowl.**

Waterproof feathers

Most waterfowl have waterproof feathers to protect them. Some birds produce a waterproof oil that they spread over their feathers with their bills.

The pelican has a flexible pouch under its bill that is used to scoop up fish.

Blue-footed boobies have webbed feet that they use to push through the water.

Other birds have different ways of keeping water out. Penguins have special feathers that overlap tightly to lock out water.

Feet like paddles

Many waterfowl have webbed feet that they use like paddles to move through the water. Other coastal birds do not have webbing. Instead, they have broad, paddlelike toes.

Scoops, spears, and strainers

The bills of coastal birds are adapted to the foods they eat. Pelicans have long, straight bills with a flexible pouch on the underside. Pelicans scoop up fish into their pouches. They may also spear fish with their bills. Other coastal birds, including flamingoes, use hairlike "combs" along the edges of the bill to strain food from the water and mud.

Diving birds

Some coastal birds dive into the water from the air to catch fish. Birds like the blue-footed booby are able to spot schools of fish from the air. The birds then draw their wings back and plunge into the water like darts. They enter the water moving so quickly that fish stand little chance of escape. Other birds dive from the surface of the water.

Fun Fact

Penguins also dive to catch their food, using their wings to swim. Penguins may dive more than 900 feet (275 meters). They can hold their breath for nearly 20 minutes!

What Birds Live Near Inland Waters?

Male mandarin ducks have brightly colored feathers to attract mates.

Inland waters are home to a wide variety of birds. These **habitats** include freshwater areas like rivers and lakes, along with saltwater areas like marshes and swamps.

Waterfowl

Like coastal birds, birds that live near inland waters have **adaptations** to life in the water. In fact, many **waterfowl** live both on coasts and near inland waters. Many waterfowl have webbed feet to move them through the water, and most have waterproof feathers.

Ducks

Ducks are found in inland waters around the world. Ducks float on the surface of the water, using their webbed feet to move. Their bills are adapted to the many different foods they eat. Some use their short, wedge-shaped bills to break open clams. Others use their bills to filter the water for insects. Male ducks tend to be brightly colored to attract females.

The blue heron has long legs for wading in the water. It uses a spearlike bill to catch fish.

Swans and geese

Swans and geese are waterfowl that are closely related to ducks. Many ducks, swans, and geese **migrate** away from areas where the water freezes. Each fall, Canada geese fill the skies of North America as they head south for the winter.

Wetlands

Wetlands are places where there is usually water near or above the surface of the ground. They provide an important habitat for many birds. Many migratory birds rely on wetlands for places to rest and feed during their long journeys.

Wading birds like cranes, flamingoes, and herons live in wetlands. They have long legs that carry their bodies above the water. They also have bills specially adapted for catching fish or filtering food from the water.

Swans use their flexible necks to feed on underwater plants.

Fun Fact

About 15 million years ago, a relative of today's ducks lived in Australia. This giant bird grew to more than 8 feet (2.4 meters) tall! Scientists have nicknamed this fearsome, flightless meat-eater the "demon duck of doom."

What Birds Live in Polar Regions?

The **polar regions** are an extreme **habitat**. These areas are so cold that they are mostly covered in snow and ice all year. They include the Arctic, which is the northernmost region of Earth; and Antarctica, an ice-buried continent that surrounds the South Pole. Many birds **migrate** to these areas during summer.

Emperor penguins are the only large animals that spend the winter in Antarctica.

Arctic summer

Winter is harsh in the Arctic, but summer brings a rich abundance of life. The sun shines all day and night during part of the summer. This plentiful sunlight causes an explosion of plant life, which in turn supports swarms of insects, herds of caribou, and millions of migrating birds. These birds include Canada geese, ducks, sandpipers, and terns, among others. Many of these birds build nests and lay eggs in the Arctic. When the days grow short at summer's end, they migrate south.

The Arctic and Antarctic are very cold regions that lie at the poles.

Antarctic summer

Antarctica is even colder than the Arctic, but it too supports migrating birds in the summer. Many sea birds nest on cliffs near the sea, feeding on the wealth

Puffins dive for fish in Arctic waters. They form large colonies during the mating season.

of sea life summer brings. Birds that flock to Antarctica in the summer include albatrosses, gulls, petrels, and skuas. These birds also migrate to avoid the winter.

Winter in polar regions

A few birds remain in polar regions through the winter. In the Arctic, ptarmigans (*TAHR muh guhns*) **molt** and grow white feathers. Their feathers provide **camouflage** against the snow and ice.

Emperor penguins are the only **vertebrates** that spend the winter in Antarctica. Penguins are well **adapted** to life in the waters around Antarctica. Their large bodies and thick coats of feathers help keep them warm. Males huddle together for warmth against the harsh wind and bitter cold, **incubating** their eggs. They take turns standing at the edge of the group, where conditions are the coldest.

Many birds migrate to the Arctic to build nests and raise their chicks.

Why Are Some Birds Endangered?

Tragically, some kinds of birds are **endangered.** Endangered animals are in danger of dying out completely. Hundreds of bird **species** are endangered, including condors, kiwis, and whooping cranes. Others are already extinct (gone forever), like the dodo, the great auk (*awk*), and the passenger pigeon.

Hunting

Some birds are endangered because human hunters are killing too many. People hunt birds for food or for their beautiful feathers. The dodo was a flightless bird about the size of a turkey that lived on an island in the Indian Ocean. Sailors killed these helpless birds for food. By 1680, the dodo was extinct.

When people cut down forests, they kill countless birds by destroying their homes.

Pollution

Birds are especially sensitive to **pollution,** or human-made chemicals that harm nature. Chemicals that are used to kill insect pests can also harm birds. A chemical called DDT kills insects but also causes bird egg shells to become too thin. This prevents chicks from hatching. DDT is especially dangerous to **birds of prey** like the California condor. Fewer than 400 of this species are alive today.

Whooping cranes may die out because people have drained many wetland habitats.

Habitat destruction

Many birds are endangered because people have damaged their **habitats.** People have cut down the forests where birds live and plowed under grasslands. Many wetlands have been drained to make room for farms. This has driven birds like the whooping crane to the edge of extinction.

Introduced animals

Birds may also be threatened by new species that people introduce. In New Zealand, birds like the kiwi are endangered because people have introduced dogs and foxes. On Gough Island in the South Atlantic, mice introduced by people eat eggs in the nests of sea birds. Several bird species on this island are near extinction.

The Tristan albatross has become endangered because introduced mice eat its chicks.

How Can We Protect Birds?

There are many ways that people can help protect the environment. Laws and treaties (agreements between countries) can make it illegal to hunt **endangered** birds. Governments can create parks and wildlife refuges to protect **habitats.** Organizations can raise money for protecting habitats and help people learn more about endangered birds. Each of us can do our part to help.

When people protect forests, they give birds like the harpy eagle a chance for survival.

Protecting birds

When people act to protect endangered birds, those animals often recover. The bald eagle disappeared from most of the United States by the 1970's because of hunting and **pollution.** Then people created laws that protected bald eagles. Now the bald eagle is no longer endangered.

Making laws

Many countries create laws or sign international treaties to protect endangered **species.** Most countries have now outlawed the spraying of the chemical DDT, which thins bird egg shells. Outlawing the use of DDT has helped birds like the California condor begin to recover.

Countries like Australia and New Zealand have created laws that prevent people from bringing in plants and animals from other countries. This helps protect birds from introduced species that may eat them or compete with them for food.

Scientists use puppets to raise condors, which are released into the wild when they are adults.

Protecting habitats

Many countries are trying to protect natural areas that are important to wildlife. Wetlands provide an important **habitat** for many birds, and countries around the world have acted to protect their wetlands. Nearly 2,000 wetlands have been protected by Australia, Canada, New Zealand, the United States, the United Kingdom, and other countries.

Doing our part

Each of us can help. Visiting wildlife refuges or zoos can teach you more about the importance of animals to the balance of nature. Reducing the amount of pollution we create can help protect habitats. Simply speaking out can help. Let others know about threats to birds, and tell them it's important that living things be protected.

Visiting wildlife refuges is educational and may help save endangered animals, too.

Activities

Bird Watching

Introduction:

Birds live almost everywhere in the world, but different kinds of birds usually live in certain regions. You can learn more about the birds in your region by observing birds in your backyard, around your neighborhood, in public parks, or just about anywhere you go. Ponds, lakes, beaches, and wetland areas are good places to spot birds.

Materials:

- Colored pencils, markers, or crayons
- Notepad or blank sheets of paper

Directions:

1. Ask a family member, teacher, or your school or public librarian to help you find books on birds that live in your region.

2. Choose an outdoor space where you can observe birds in their natural **habitat.** If you live in a region that gets very cold, you are more likely to see birds in the spring, summer, or early fall.

3. Use your school or library book to try to identify the kinds of birds that you see. Find out if the bird lives in your region the year around, or if it **migrates** to another region. You can also write down the names of the birds you see and draw pictures of them to create your own guide.

4. What do you notice about the birds that you see? You may want to answer questions like:
   - Were the birds in trees, on the ground, or some other place?
   - How many birds were there?
   - What were the birds doing?

5. Take your notebook with you whenever you're outside. If you see a new bird, make a sketch of it in your notebook so you can look up its name later on.

Endangered Birds Research Project

Introduction:

Many kinds of birds are **endangered** because of human activities or other causes. The best way to protect endangered animals is to tell other people about the threats to these animals. You can find out more about endangered birds in your region or country by looking up information in your school or public library.

Materials:

• Poster board

• Markers

Directions:

1. Ask a family member, teacher, or your school or public librarian to help you find information on endangered birds in your region or country.

2. Choose a bird that you wish to learn more about. Write down important information about the bird and why it is endangered. Questions you may wish to answer include:

   • Where does this bird live?

   • What is unique about the bird?

   • What is the bird's natural habitat?

   • What are the main threats to this bird?

   • What are people doing to help protect the bird?

3. Draw a picture of the bird on the poster board. Write down information about the bird you'd like to share with others. You can present what you found out to your class, family, or friends.

The piping plover is an endangered bird of North America.

Glossary

adaptation; adapted a feature or trait that helps a living thing survive in its environment; fitted.

bird of prey any one of a group of birds, including eagles, hawks, owls, and vultures, that hunt animals and eat their flesh.

camouflage (n.) special coloring or texture that helps an animal blend in with its environment; (v.) to look like something else in order to hide.

colony a group of animals or plants of the same kind, living or growing together.

courtship the courting or wooing of a female animal by a male.

endangered in danger of dying off completely.

habitat a place where a plant or animal lives in the wild.

incubate to sit on eggs in order to hatch them.

life cycle the stages of development that a living thing passes through.

mammal an animal that feeds its young on the mother's milk.

migrate; migration to move from one region to another; the movement of animals to a place that offers better living conditions.

molt to shed feathers, skin, hair, a shell, or other growths, before a new growth.

nocturnal active at night.

polar regions areas of bitterly cold land and ocean that lie at the northernmost and southernmost parts of Earth.

pollution all the ways that human activity harms nature.

predator a hunting animal.

prey any animal or animals hunted for food by another animal.

reproduce to make more of something.

scavenger an animal that feeds on decaying matter.

species a group of animals or plants that have certain permanent characteristics in common and are able to breed with one another.

talon the claw of an animal, especially a bird of prey.

territory an area that an animal claims and defends as its own.

vertebrate an animal with a backbone.

warm-blooded having blood that almost always stays about the same temperature no matter what the temperature of the animal's surroundings are.

waterfowl a water bird, especially one that swims.

Find Out More

Books

The Bird Class by Rebecca Stefoff (Benchmark Books, 2008)

Learn about each family of birds, their physical features, life cycles, behavior, habitats, and conservation issues.

Birds: Nature's Magnificent Flying Machines by Caroline Arnold (Charlesbridge, 2003)

This book explains how different kinds of wings help different kinds of birds survive.

Everything Bird: What Kids Really Want to Know About Birds by Cherie Winner (NorthWord Books, 2007)

Many of your questions about birds will be answered here, such as why vultures are so ugly and whether woodpeckers ever get headaches from all their pecking.

Grzimek's Student Animal Life Resource: Birds by Bernhard Grzimek and Melissa C. McDade (UXL, 2005) 5 volumes

This encyclopedia gives basic information on everything you ever want to know about every kind of bird.

The Young Birder's Guide to Birds of Eastern North America by Bill Thompson (Houghton Mifflin, 2008)

If you live in the eastern part of North America, this guidebook will help you in bird watching and bird identification.

Web sites

All About Birds

http://www.enchantedlearning.com/subjects/birds/

A special feature of this Web site is the sidebar menu, which offers selections to such categories as "Bird Extremes," "Bird Watching," and "Birds and People."

Bird Feeder Cam

http://www.wbu.com/feedercam_home.htm

Wild Birds Unlimited has set up cameras at several different bird feeders, so you can watch birds arrive, eat, and depart right from your own computer.

National Geographic Kids: Animals Creature Features

http://kids.nationalgeographic.com/Animals/CreatureFeature

Click on "Birds" in the menu to learn about the Adélie penguin, Atlantic puffin, bald eagle, blue-footed booby, Canada goose, emperor penguin, Indian peafowl, ostrich, peregrine falcon, pileated woodpecker, red-tailed hawk, snowy owl, and tundra swan.

U.S. Fish & Wildlife Service: Kids' Corner

http://www.fws.gov/endangered/kids/

The focus is on how you can get involved in saving our wildlife and conserving their natural habitats.

Index